The Last Clear Narrative

ALSO BY RACHEL ZUCKER

Eating in the Underworld (Wesleyan, 2003)

The Last Clear Narrative

RACHEL ZUCKER

Wesleyan University Press

Middletown, Connecticut

Published by Wesleyan University Press, Middletown, CT 06459

Printed in the United States of America

Design by Joy Katz

Set in Vectora and Futura types by BW&A Books, Inc.

Library of Congress Cataloging-in-Publication Data

Zucker, Rachel.

The last clear narrative / by Rachel Zucker.

p. cm.

ISBN 0-8195-6710-8 (cloth : alk. paper)

ISBN 0-8195-6711-6 (pbk. : alk. paper)

1. Motherhood—Poetry. 2. Mother and child—Poetry. I. Title.

PS3626.U26L36 2004

811'.6—dc22

2004049605

5   4   3   2   1

first, my husband

then, my sons

o

and for my great-aunt

Marguerite "Snoekie" Gutwirth Stolz

1914–1999

[CONTENTS]

The Last Clear Narrative

A KIND OF CATASTROPHE

        about this snow I'd say
little,
        less than necessary,
                it's so
readily available for metaphor or
        melting

is not the same as
        transcendence, transformation,
  erosion—

not sure what it means,
who we might be without these
        forms
define us whether or not we willingly
conform, assert some
        desperate arrogance—

and speaking of moons: I don't believe,
necessarily, there was one.

        For example;

. . . when the narrator says he's lost
consciousness, is dreaming of
his mother maybe
his first memory his
birth—I tend to doubt
his hazy reportage.

He says *and now a word about . . .*
but obviously means more than one.

He says *a fake ceiling* and means
a real ceiling made out of something
other than what other ceilings are made out of.

       The snow is not going anywhere

doesn't mean it isn't coming down and
even if I knew what color   exactly
the sky blanked out to doesn't mean
I'd tell you
      or could tell you
except by way of saying
                  something
else—   something
      close to what I mean—
something,
      not like a mirror to my soul
and not like looking *at* but seeing
      the backing painted not plated
silver, worthless, altogether—

this doesn't mean I don't remember—

(the snow a window the child we did not conceive that night I saw
you then this is another winter that's still my picture the harsher
elements and our beginning or starting to love and love)   you

probably remember it differently.

Whose place is it to say what happened?

      The snow is not a symbol but literal.

You happened
            and happen to be here—
    where I am
    which changes and is always,
from my point of view, first person.

I'm not the narrator or speaker,
      make a mess of omens:

       This snow

doesn't mean anything;

     I suppose you're sleeping and may be seeing
something else entirely
        or nothing—

Sometimes you say
   don't make too much of it.

It is just snow.

      I try putting lilacs in your dream
   but can't be sure you'll see them;
      they're so far out of season,
        I can't make them make sense.

About this snow I'd say

you're sleeping and are as beautiful this night
                        as that night and that night and
        that night in New Haven

            when the snow came down
and I didn't make too much of it—
        was—   we were,

            in it
        the moment
                        I made a picture of
                to look at later—

    now
    you're different—   here—

                        (I never imagined)

                    three winters later—

o

[MARRIAGE IS]

allegory.

please tell me how will you read this
or, by not reading, establish

sympathy for the characters

    plot progression?
    rising action?

(closed system

"sanctity"   "sacrament"   "sacrifice"

require other types

    of animal husbandry

        s -- on request)

the tank expands to fit

this swelling tide of detail
nothing outside

our circle of attention

[REGISTRY]

how are the brackets working in this section?

music!

hegemony, inevitably
bowls in different colors

to say *the other is* or *this spoon's too big for the human mouth* is

exchange for equal value
settings-for-eight

no one can predict
the need for crystal or delicate

[W E D D I N G]

(the beauty of it)

a play we made

benefit others donate a

who's to say if   *we're well suited for* —— *italic fragments, collage-like*

fund means more than

resources imply

resilience or resistance to

like antibodies

we accrue

a kind of interface, *god's sake,*

appearance of:

at once, the leading lady, *& conversely here I expect the poem to continue when I turn the page*

[PROPRIETY]   *title play* →

in French the word "propre"

cleanliness ~~in a sense~~ *calls attention to the making*
ownership

some men like
some men like

even a woman has certain

in the old days, she unraveled and
suitors, kept at bay, regarded her

no one spoke of   [ ]

~~you~~ only own ~~your~~ own

this brocade ~~untouched by human~~ ──────────── (wish)

and in the other room

raveling, unraveling kept

[PROPERTY]

erasing the subject, creates distance

from a distance ~~you~~   can't discern

red plaid hat dense thicket

"don't
          shoot! my husband

when not at home, the house

privacy

the story demands

looms, idle hands, wonders, *what's a woman*   ?

a woman to

oo

WHITEWASH

Through the window a man is moving.

I learn and learn his form
        from room to room to room.

As a child, the elevator opened onto a similar but
significant scene;   someone said:

        we're here.

Later I learn *up* and *down* without windows,
small jolt on takeoff.

                Going up?

Where is the backyard?
Where is the back door?
Why is the City still hanging around?

It used to be the crawlspace was filled with animals
and looking (up) meant something.

Winter slowing down.

Now there are a limited number of gestures.
A thing done is change or an arrangement.

AT NIGHT

        I could pretend to miss an ex-lover
      for comfort or to pass the time, remember
how I loved and was not loved back while
     the back of my husband is not like the back
of my hand and not like the back-handed
    comment and not like
        what I expected

if I lean all the way over I see
     the moon
just above the buildings which think
    they're fences: all surface,
      meant to be containers

when I lie back it is not there

    just the space against the space
        against his back

a low divider rising up in the highway

avoiding your mother's eye on 6th avenue

walking right by, she never noticed

do you promise to keep looking at the world?

but vows are impossible, untrustworthy, desirous, *liar!*

this disappointment in yourself a lens through which you see the world and once

> a field of fireflies your husband wakes you up to see within this frame of disappointment so that—the opposite of dreaming—you wake up finally see—a new (no name yet) frame—it's gone (the disappoint-ment) that vignetted all you saw (burning in the edges, narrowing in your subject) and instead, now, the field of fireflies too far past dusk for color, just light and motion, a shifting, impossible light and motion brief lucid—you don't even have a take on this—your husband who was not your husband but will be, wakes you and the car roughs up the gravel and settles on the shoulder of the road

pray

not to be the kind of person who doesn't wake up

or who wakes up and says "the jewel is India" or "the air strike is preemptive"

animals, mountains, people, certain people who seem certain or love animals

say *this is my mother* and don't grimace

part of why your husband loves you is he loves women

look how his chest hair sneaks up out of his collar

nights,

drawn together

a kind of

repeating analogy

how I wish I was not so

afraid :   animals, numbers, my mother,

my mother's mother

oh no,

there is that slim moon
in the five again

hanging
from the simple hook—look,

it doesn't even need a noose, that moon,

it always hangs there

In your version of heaven I am blond, thinner,
but not so witty. In the movie version of your version
of heaven you fight God to come back to me.
It is a box office hit because you are an unbelievable character.
Nothing is real except the well-timed traffic accident
which costs 226 thousand dollars.

In real life, I am on a small bridge over a small creek.
Then it isn't a bridge but a stadium. Then a low table.
A sense of knowing the future.
There is no clear location of fear.
I want you to say you will abandon your dissertation.
I want you to ask the man in the green scrubs if I was pregnant.

Put on the preservers! they announce. *They are under your seats!*
Time to tell your wife a few last things. People are puking
in the rows around us. The jackets sweaty and too big.
We are, in this version, an image of hope.
The broadcasters are just now sniffing us out.
I am pregnant but don't know it and can't know
the fetus would have been, in any event, not viable.
No one survives. No one comes down with cancer.
The fade-out leaves a black screen over the sound of water.

The review says it is a *film noir.* The letter to the editor
says the reviewer should go back to college. The reviewer
is in graduate school writing a thesis about movies
that were never made. If they are made he will not get tenure.
If we die he has a small chance at success. A young woman
writes in: *it should, more properly, have been called an embryo*.

WHEN I KNOCK ON THE WALL OF THE NEXT STANZA

the neighbor answers
by shouting back
the secret name my lover calls me during sex

once giants roamed the earth and delicate maidens
shot them through the heart with sharpened reeds

the water wanted to go one way
but the current wanted to go another

how can it?

the current *is* the way the water wants to go
or is it?

oo
o

I read the instructions twice and pee on my hand by mistake.
I wait.
I try again and then, in the 2 minutes 15 seconds it takes to get the First Response
I watch Ponch deliver a baby in a trailer the CHiPs pulled over for speeding.
The woman's screaming.
Ponch pours water from a canteen over his hands and kneels between her legs.
Thirty-five seconds later he emerges from the trailer, pulls on black leather
gloves, there's no blood, and
one pink bar
on the plastic view screen.

TRYING TO REASSURE YOU (7 WEEKS)

If you were a woman
I'd wear your lipstick.

You pull away so quickly.

Apricot and *abricot*.
We're not so different.

I wait and wait until I cannot (wait)   *implies eventual movement*
and then I take gold bands

from the lion's mouth,
lie beneath his mane

and (stay.)   *surprise*

STARS AND SUNS OF MY BODY (10 WEEKS)

Rays etch out along my breasts like frightened trails
or tracks of a small mouse in the snow looking for heat—
back and back to the thin center where the pipe leaks
steam from the basement dryer up onto the ground.
How will he ever get down?

I'm not scared to death just scared
not frightened of my shadow—only
the shape of the shadow I can't
hear time or the blinking heart
what lies what is what changes?

The child doesn't visit in dreams
I have no way of knowing
am not ready only a woman
waiting   for the shadow
to fit, slip out a hard portrait
bony man-baby, bright spot
on the new map

BEING MARKED OR OBVIOUS (18 WEEKS)

Others know or think something of me my recent activities
the supermarket bagger smiles, shakes her head
security guard says congratulations I walk by
I've never seen these people pass little nods
and phrases my way they know or think they know
something of my recent future are we a club?
not secret a kind of coven   try to smile back
but there's no one you are an image on a tape in a VCR
but are not you have kidneys a liver bladder I'd like to
meet you at some scenic overlook look around
we'd know we saw the same moment on the edge
of something sometimes there's a guardrail or a guard
or just the view keeping you back, solitude, I wish you
were here although you are   I am the fish around
the hand around the fist of DNA   my body pools
it tides outside the terrible sounds of cars and children
after school then a silent long space and voices closing
in again around—I carefully house what I cannot see

In DC, the nasal monitor was pulled out through the nose.

The journal entry: "12:37—Severe pain . . ."

          Under the coffee table. alone.

grounded in place

They say *she looked peaceful.*

What does peaceful look like?

_____

(, Bosnia, Massada, Rwanda,)

It is better to look dead than be dead.

The one who would survive did not look peaceful but no one can testify—got up out of the ditch himself and moved on; (they were gone) no one there to say what he looked like.

He is stronger, cared for, saved; they videotape and record the details.

(DC)

They found her—monitor pulled up, out up, through the nose—medical journal for recording—it was a simple procedure, went home alone not like her not to call, they went to find

and found her

(NY)

The heartbeat makes it alive—monitor shows the beat, blips, blinking—mechanical, visual sound

two sacs side by side.

[bip, bip-bip, bip, bip-bip]

(Oh Jesus Christ.)

(DC)

Today, you will see the still-frail witness's picture in the paper and not care. You will go to her funeral in Toledo where the parents behave badly because no one can find the will.

You lose a lavender sweater. You lose the black sweater. You lose two T-shirts, a watch and two important books.

---

switch in perspective

(NY)

In the dream my plane goes down again.

Then it goes down again.

The 747 headlong through Central Park.
       pell-mell—! heedless—! speeding mass in unison—!

*the comma's disruption of rhythm,
how it slows*

Something's, just, not, right—

       he's thick-necked, slow speaking.

(NY)

My dead grandmother tells me not to make a collage of tragedy.
They are not the same, she says.

Suffering's not one substance.

(NY)

On the monitor: a heartbeat, fetal movement—only one.
The doctor holding her breath.
The monitor: one—jellied controls slide easily over, my breath inside—

(he: *we were only trying for one*—)

*ultra*sound

that's *my* heart

(face to one side, lying
"mass"

Dr. doesn't answer when I *what is it what's wrong with why isn't*—

I love this moment, how it acts momentarly as contradiction

One can't say, the doctor says *dead* exactly—after all would you say your liver is alive? kidneys?

The procedure surprised us but not much—

      (the plane went down and stayed down)

and the fetus, single twin with heart, is what later I say—moving enormous head on skeletal body—looks peaceful

(pay phone)

How can I say it will be easier to get up tomorrow?
I don't know where the sweaters are.

I would help you look but am in New Haven watching women—their careful eating,
pressed clothes, sharpened utensils—trying to prepare a lecture: description in poetry.

How can I say it will be easier——?

(the witness trying to tell us—)

(your voice, when you first call

[*hello?*]

is: (not yet not yet) still a ragged tremble—
breath in an earthquake, a nervous bell about
to ring or the sound of the ninth chime when
you don't know what time it is—

Is it 10 o'clock?
Is it 11?

)

witness: a bridal quilt should not be slept on, or under

witness: to sign, watch, guard, (a ram's horn)

witness: My great aunt Ida and her husband hired a guide to lead them over the Alps. When they came to a clearing the guide said dig. And you know what they dug. Jewelry sewn into the lining. Side-by-side plot. Her father the Rabbi in Africa, waiting. Sons all over the Far East and Europe. Books buried in his backyard. I have a suitcase of photos of dead Jews. Photos of Jews that made it to America, photos of Ida's wedding, circa 1920.

witness: one reason I stop working on 47th Street is the black hats get out of the elevator when I enter. woman alone. witness! witness! what if only one survivor?

danger! woman.

ovum: as an egg gets big the shell must thicken to support the structure but then he can't breathe through it; e.g., the dinosaur and her tiny egg

embryo: a developing human from implantation to the end of the eighth week
fetus: a developing human from three months after conception to birth

> in between something happened or stopped happening; one twin bigger and moving and one—well everything changed when we learned to look inside the body, what we saw little armies of corpuscles and arteries and nerve endings we called them cells and viruses and neurotransmitters and this made us compassionate and develop weapons, spacious waiting rooms, who knows how many twins conceived reach the fetal stage, midwives used a funnel-shaped tool pressed up against the belly

to father: to wait outside, "Sir . . . your wife, . . .
when something is wrong: to father: to be made to be patient

mass: fibroid, benign, collection of cells not necessarily anything

        undress, he said in French and motioned to your sweater, off
        in America the doctor leaves the room you do not say
        his fingers around the node, the mass, your hand above your head
        reclining
        the size is not important he said
        not relevant? not massive? not diagnostic?

        trifling, minor, these too are lesser masses

mass: tumor on the adrenal gland misdiagnosed as panic misdiagnosed as heartburn
    my mother-in-law's best friend: Randy Goldman, died (D.C.) age 50

mass: that same Yom Kippur we left temple, undressed hurriedly, made love, slept, conceived a child

mass: a people moving across continents: arrowhead, crockery, Pentateuch, Talmud

holocaust overcast.

(mass, to father)

        tinged like a raw climate.

            Scheveningen, 1920. Anvers, 1928. San Moritz, 1935.

Ryglice. Paris.   Auschwitz.   or

        Africa. Cuba. New York.

Have I mentioned his books buried in the backyard? Have I mentioned the photo of Gutmann and Chaya on the balcony, in the open, his white beard, her blind eyes; or in the garden or on the veranda—

Harry and Albert, the brothers Kleinhaus, have a slot in the wall of their offices for passing diamonds. *Look at this!* Harry calls out. *Look at this, Albert.*

No one can describe the absolute white light of the trilliant. That's why they're diamonds, why people buy them. That's why, when the Jews were rounded up and stripped and herded, robbed and slaughtered, the light was nothing to save them. and at first no one believed it.

unlike a Greek myth, the ground around Gutmann's books was dirt. nothing in there to look for or become and the books survived and were sent to America where almost everyone survives   die of old age, of cancer, of missing his wife

I have a suitcase of photos of dead Jews.

but no one to tell of my lost baby—
  and no one to pray for the one I carry—   tiny sons.

filament, cilium, I am attached too fragily to history

witness: when you encounter the Torah, kiss it. with the fringes of your shawl, the tips of your fingers, the spine of your prayerbook. I have even seen men touch lips to the cover.

in love with parchment.

people in mass graves, air-raids, bombing, the man with a machine gun on the corner, jets quaking the sky so the president can throw out the first pitch of the series. as I write this we are bombing and rounding up as you read this who knows what we have thought of so many ways to murder, to birth, to memory, to meaning

the next line of this poem I delete in the revision: ⚹

                but is still there in echo, my neural net, the deleted what is white space

so few ways to murder, birth, memory,

(mass: the fetal tissue of the lost twin is reabsorbed by the body (my body) in the next two trimesters
within the mother,   the body

mass: the moment the ovum infiltrated, inspired)

      and is there, in echo, what is white

but unlike the man painted over in Vermeer's *Maid Asleep* (the man and little dog in the nearest doorway) there
is no radiograph to reveal it—   this   when I die

disappears

RATHER A STRUCTURE OR PROCESS (21 WEEKS)

                              —he's kicking or

can't tell could be fists don't need electronic pictures
punch, flutters, doesn't belong to me
not my body I think *do you like apples?*
                    Do you like jelly? I chew
carefully meanwhile my genitals a one-way exit
flash way-out-this-way I'm all process, a short epoch

The bird on the sill looks in and flies away
before the husband shoos. The phone is many voices,
tones, trebles, names but all the same. It says
he could survive outside the womb. It says
you're in the homestretch now then doesn't ring
for hours. I'd like to describe myself as she
but am only myself and you—not separate
or symbiotic; I keep you alive. Once I said
to my idea: bide awhile then come farther
into the world. But right away you were not mine
or me—a tiny Jonah, fleshy Pinocchio.
                   Today I read: *the organs*
have just stopped showing through the skin
and imagine your bones like reeds or thin switches.
Waiting for sugar to form candy crystals,
for what you are to stick. Once I made, or should I say
constructed, brandy from vodka, rock candy
and unripe peaches. I canned the extra peaches into jams
and butters, saved a few well past safe eating to look at
and remember summer. But I spared nothing to make you
and have nothing left.   loss of self, Plath's "Morning Song"

THISTLE, OR LETTER FOR MY HUSBAND (33 WEEKS)

Do you have a spare self or shadow to keep me cool
take off this dreadful skin, future pressing in, the present humid, slippery
you know your wife too big used to be me but I espy your dream
of women never thin enough   if I could photograph myself
out of this, be a man writing about animals or history, extinct fauna,
husked mollusks but I can't. Look how the months swing by and taunt me—
                                        Oh! I'm attached!
one day will be a cloth monkey—but I swear, I will not be done to.
I will not be a smooth oyster waiting for nacre to coat my unseens, despair
polishing, bending light through me. Instead I'd sell my long hair
for a few mother-of-pearl buttons, unclasp my heart from its open birdcage
but not put desire away, I'll not put desire away. Remember: I am inside who I was.

transformation, wholeness

It's not what you suspect.

      (Taking a taxi home for no reason.
✳   Leaving the movie early. Who is it
      I'm talking to on the phone, in the
      room, in the end, where do I go?)

      The essay is too easy
to dissemble. The sentence
      sickens, then dismisses:

The boy with two arms is not an amputee.

I leave the ring on the nightstand.

There is a will under the pillow.

ooo
o

SONNET NON-VOLTA

This morning I woke with four pre-war buildings on my chest.

Now it hurts to breathe.

The architect-signature cornerstone, an etched gray slab, rests dangerously close to my septum.

The falling bricks and modernized penthouse—the roof chairs, impatiens, La-Z-Boys, kitchenettes,
baby grands, kiddish cups, bunkbeds, iguana tanks, faux-marble coffee table, and thousands
of pounds of *The New York Times*.

I am afraid to turn over.

Blue jays peck at my fire-escape basil.

A chandelier falls in one of the lobbies killing a child, a retriever and a young nanny.

The doormen rush about, tripping on rain mats, tipping over silk geraniums.

My breasts are the only things between balance and avalanche.

I try short, shallow breathing, but it's too heavy.

Just then you appear in the doorway. It's time to go, you say, dressed and ready,

and stand there calling me by the wrong name.

THE WINDOW IS ONE-SIDED IT DOES NOT ADMIT

when will I measure my life
         by the by or sentence again

                  (a pace a pace)

this red-faced hunger lonely startled almost asleep he

                                    unmeasures me

I am a thin stain   watery white mark
         my hand against the glass

     the breast another breast

and the city licked over with haze doesn't notice I'm waving and waving

so much space, I assume
an ending

sway the baby, cup the back, unfurl the little legs

I simian long to be all-legged swing him
                    clutch-clutch
                            clutch-clutch
          if you can the shadow of wild smells

and where is my lost wherewithal?
  stubborn body.

I am leaving and weaving the room into smaller rations of air
          hands around the spiny parcel   the cry
                    undoing years   the self tracery   (efface, efface)

                    the cries make piece-work of me

(pace pace)

who measures my losing my slip the sure erasure
we are liquid, body, breast, a tiny shower the cry enters I

am veined

with the cry —

can anyone get inside this crying we make glazes the city the soft glass
                                                    it, I, invisible
        no linguistic for this:
    the city, my gesture, soon the dawn I have seen so many measures up

        I carve   active, violent, physical

                                            space!

                                    days,   days

days

and I said to anyone can only see his

red face fists too tight   I somehow taught him

hunger, impatience, every minute a measure of my
                 must must must erase the getting there and just

be   the thin stain he swallows and clings

the door swings: visitor, family, enter act II with another and another
mother they examine his private some men
hold knees apart I make a speech with what words and

cut—blood as many gauze

the city is dangerous

repelling the window   is vertigo is stasis is itself fallen

dream: cry, suck, cry
awake: we are a seam ironed open for strength

the window one-sided   view irrelevant

it is the edges that measure

(cry, suck, cry)

returning

one day

I will gather a story to tell you

                            what night looked like
what every city vista told day and day
          heat and time   was not, were no
I knew you were   I knew there was you

          and summer and never any other season

THE RISE IN THE AVENUE

Instinct says I am smelled out,   *known, seen, caught*
the untoothed hunter knows my slow frame.

The baby sucks the inner elbow, right wrist,
hand holding the pen until another poem
is rocked out into the afternoon,   *like a child, soothed & nurtured*
into the city swallowing minions.

At night, all the missing is taken up—space
that used to be back to back or back to front or
front to front (knees interlocking)—now a gentle bumper
lest we overlay what once we made. Meanwhile hunger
followed by famine: his face a graphic error for hatred.

I'm tired of watching for changes,
macrophages, sudden death or threat
of suffocation. I've been promoted
master of homeostasis: maintain, sustain, pattern.

And look how even the asphalt intercedes—
these non-sequitur days, their lilting, lifting shape—
as I wait for what I can't see coming.
                looming

he has a range is almost out of hand
by day demands the keep-away accident
waiting to happen how did this child become
volitional? at night almost out of ambivalence
beside myself we're eyes roosting
our one desire to be   satisfied
even cribbed his cry my tiny master *emergency*
seems the woman I was has gone missing
again no matter rocking makes it later and later
he presses a wet-chin smile to my ear
and in the early winter claims it's morning
I pull the shade up off the avenue, my eye
softens, see: he's why I will not want to die

HAVING A BABY, ATOM BOMB

three months later a friend has a baby describes the labor now we have babies have babies and nothing in common perhaps the bomb on two unsimilar landscapes different patterns disaster a stupid simile like when someone says from space it all looks the same as if and my body a blasted crater the sounds of my house in fact all this the bomb too big to escape this-specific-day I want to outlive and the space between bathroom and bedrooms one hand against each door this used to be a study sense him breathing means he lives, sleeps, this way station called hallway arm's length apart the walls from space collapse to nothing, less than

NOT KNOWING NIJINSKY OR DIAGHILEV

A certain kind of man asks the same question
again, again until it isn't a question but
      a threat, shove, spit in the eye.
Phyllis says *you're sitting on your power* but
I know what I'm sitting on: my ass. Obviously,
running out of language.

My desire is "a pre-electric impulse with a too-small synapse."
What a tired image that is. I sit on my power.

Finally, in the boxed-up city, night comes on
without a sunset; books push out their backs,
turn stiff arms away, press closer together.

    The editor says: *we have no patience for metaphor.*

In the dream the baby carrier is crammed with plastic bags.
My ex-lover shoots hockey pucks at my breasts through a metal tube.
I want to hold you once before the world explodes I say to the baby
who is not there. Two women screaming "Filthy Jews!" die too.

    The memo from the editor: *it is even sub-Hollywood.*

I sit on my power and try to describe anything.

"My mother inside me": air in a well; a heavy, starless chill.
Her love the texture of canned lotus root, the color
a cross-section of diseased lung; slight smell of vinegar.

The editor jots: *no patience for description*.

So I'm back where I started; another old man and his helpful invective.

He suspects me. Uses the words "musicality," "mimesis";
     what do you know, if anything?

I think: I know what it is to have a child . . . but (truth is) not now, I only know
               what it is like.

Here: here is a picture of me in labor:

    . . . hand around the metal bar the body
   crushing in and in the room white-hot,
          exploding

The reason I even mention   [it]   is that I don't know anything
but memory which is nothing except—child, sleeping in my elbow—
marks and tracings, a neural map, my thoughts are like piranha,
transparent and vicious, but no one gets away with similes like that.
Where is the pool of diction the myth described? The old man
spits in my eye, says *a child is no excuse* and points, pushing me
toward the shallow pond.

o
ooo
o

the I alone, writing, wanting, the winter sun false, furious

        but not   the writing   wanting   sun   only   she
in the mind without mind—as in [I want] her [to live forever] is what I want
    you to see as in red riding hood on the way to the old
woman (thought *must remembe*r) saw [she] in her mind along
    the big road men use, the mother's words making a thin
shroud around the old [she] woman—an orange tartan in summer—
    still alive inside the girl no longer in the house

the notion of performance
feels especially alive here,
attention to the "I" -choice
what the writer chooses to share,
what she wants you to see

65

I.   in Hebrew *bilvi* as in

little red riding hood through the woods to see the old woman said *bilvi* "must remember, must remember the words my mother . . ." and (good girl!) took the big road traveled by many men—

bilvi : to myself or, literally, "in my heart"

"I want you to live"   in [my heart] not for [my self]

II. description doesn't help

                              I want to explain not show but it isn't
          possible [you]   have only my word   perhaps her photo possibly
empathy but that brings so many interlopers into   the apartment, between us
          on the horseshoe-shaped beige couch—get out!—she's quiet still
          alive
                         I want to sit a minute more her
                                                    this memory
a too hot room her under the orange tartan I sweating in floral maternity—leave us

                         alone

III.   I wanted her to live forever.

is not an expression of

self, my anything   I wanted her to live.

IV. "if only"

but language cannot help   rope bridge to the wrong village

V.   the gate was already unlocked

                          left open   philosophers have been here and poets
and all kinds of thinkers picked their way years ago around the house for family photos
            self portraits shards crockery diaries   to express self or not self
to unimagine the house it-self is no new idea

                    she death tremendous not unusual

                        so don't *use* it

            she   to express   others are   not an expression of
        my or interiority   not even the balloon or plastic bag caught up
in air currents above the buildings   is emblematic

            my loneliness separate   from everything

VI.   I would be the wolf that swallows

            the little girl brings bread and meat or soup and drink or so the story goes
the old woman (in one version a grandmother in another not) hasn't got a chance
        the old woman hasn't got soup or bread meat or drink or any chance

           in this case she stopped eating long even before death
    it was a relief not to bother the pancreatic had the upper hand she was feeding
the wrong beast still not to come *à table* was unusual not even clear broth
    bread   eventually ice chips

        the details in different versions

VII. The wolf smelled her out her age itself foreshadowing and the forest
           obvious   foolish girl, ("must remember") words won't

           must must remember want her   to—

in the last days the tartan I can't help describe remember I was so big she always said *when is it when is the baby what day do you* but couldn't finish—meanwhile he was kicking and I was trying to cook him faster and push him out to see she barely made a mark along the horseshoe beige couch so thin from not even broth just ice chips a straw of water I wanted her to stay to be forever and she stayed and she stayed and she took water through a straw, disappearing the ice chips her lips too dry to say what would she anyway until the baby in her arms last time I saw she almost just a bony cage body what we call human no longer describes and I took the baby and weak myself went away just two days I wanted her to live and live to stay not just see him but be there when I wanted her to be not emblematic not life-process but alive

           months

she

only inside

the orange tartan, too hot room; it is now

November on the big road used by many men

would I were the wolf and she inside

(whole; no mind; alive)

would I could describe but have only my, I, body

wish: "I wanted her to live"

and the child and you know nothing of it

this terrible swallow I suffer I long to open show

she

here is a thin pencil

come, woodcutter

split me down the center

ooo
oo
o

THE ARGUMENT WAS SIMPLE

"don't."

but it has gone out of fashion
to describe

for example: when I tell you this sadness it does not
make you sad nor does this anger make you sorry

femoral, radial, subclavian

and where is the river but on the stones and nearby leaves
a darker green where it passed by

my son's thumbprint on the lens of my camera
my eyes in that photo after our wedding

It used to be that generations died for nothing
but old age or, otherwise, tragedy. We have
no right to address history. No right to prefer
a father to a mother. A husband to a friend.

Peaches over plums. For so began the bombings.
Let the slamming door miss your close attention.
If he dresses his heart with mayonnaise instead of
lemon-butter it is none of your business. This

sickness of looking proves addictive. It eclipses
slavery, suffrage, the chambers. Meanwhile,
I wear my own hair without a thought. I make
lists of the damned and outside, they all change

jobs. I watch through binoculars as they all
change jobs. An infant screams the double-bleating
wail of hunger, then quiets when a breast appears
from somewhere. Just another ice cream truck

under the window. Planes keeping the sky
involved. Women losing weight after the first
child. By now too many people have touched
all the fruits and vegetables so no one knows

how the drug got out of vials they were saving
for special occasions. We just suddenly noticed
everything dusted in saffron but still so inexpensive.
Ask your father what his father did for a living—

what happened when the factories were converted.
How they all made money back in the day,
back in the days when the brown bettys were good
though the apples looked less perfect.

you're so small you said *I wish that*   / collosus
I could live inside your ear.

Perhaps by that time I was dreaming.

Mostly, I'm so close I cannot see you.
My view includes your chest to eyebrows
which reminds me that I'm shorter
though when in bed we're equal if
you sleep with feet just off the mattress.

John and Paula called last week from Patmos.
They'd just finished a big puzzle of a city at night.
John did the black parts and Paula put the picture together.   grounding in naming,
                                                                 creation of a world

Then Joan called but I wasn't home.

                    Doug calls—

Months later, at a wedding, I watch you
help the cousins bouncing Mindy high.
Women dance around, around and I
understand, at last, what marriage is.
The cruelest kind of love. People
we care for are dying. But I hear
only you. You live inside my ear.

DESPITE REPORTS, CURIOUS GEORGE NOT A MONKEY, HAS NO TAIL

> *What things know no one knows*
> —Lyn Hejinian

how the *s* changes passersby
inside like a fetus makes mother what was
woman

on the local you pass with your express
                    a human in neon biosuit
that corner of your eye reserved for
tailed afflictions, pale-skinned angels—shudders, flinches

"fever 102° no daycare"
"vomit, day three, no daycare"

meanwhile our thick-waisted planet like a roast pig basking

puffins and penguins are birds that swim
the seal a torpedo upside down

husband, various complaints, wants sex, also

and they are scanning my motherhood

I want to say *wait on the front steps* but haven't any
want to say get out so I can stare at this wall as I was born to do

but when I say so the machine colors the image a solid boysenberry
and an ovoid region above my pelvis blinks beige . . . black . . . beige . . .

the technician's higher level of education makes his
diagnosis no more true than *the shapes in a balloon are?*

lake above canal
grape on a skirtless broom
a letter we'll call "o-on-i"
penelope over odysseus
cloud and spear

VIVIPARITY

the spoke holds the wheel's intelligence but controls nothing
like the spine aware of danger tightens but cannot move
these limbs have so much power

behold the downed perimeter and beyond
the frail-limbed fathers bringing things in ziploc baggies

meanwhile I must get up and make his childhood /creation
up, up this steep embankment of no sleep
to sort stones from snail shells though
he is too young to count or fathom matters

just one moment, please, I beg to conjure:
the neck of the lute
the rim of the glass
the way the wheel eventually stops without knowing

FIVE DAYS ON FIRE ISLAND, OR "MARRIAGE OPENS A PANEL ON A LACQUERED BOX"

It [marriage] is no use and no use describing.
Yours is nothing like this.
Even my husband's marriage is nothing like this.

Try to rhyme two words after the fact by rubbing them together—
spark, spark, nothing . . . in this damp clime it seems
rhyming's out of season.

Along the boardwalk our naked soles grab and reject,
splinter. Skin and wood and heavy walking;
what did you expect?

I mean to say nothing of where we're going,
the breeze off the ocean, our neglected sandals.

What brought us is misleading
just as all comparisons yield meaning.

Marriage, varnished wood, bare feet on weathered slats.

Not philosophy so much as a confession:
one thing sticks to another but explains nothing.

MY FRIEND LEAVES HIS WIFE AND TWO YOUNG CHILDREN AND SEE HOW I ABUSE HIM WITH MY TITLE

Sometimes I write a line so good I can't be sure it's mine
and the poem never feels right
not right without it either

the mind a sticky thing assailed by orphan phrases

     "there she was"

               or
"I was looking"

                  _____

Even in my dream my own screaming for help annoys me

my son's leg severed clean off his body; leg joint shiny like a cleaned chicken

and I envy

your loneliness
the sound of your empty shack

I feel like myself again you said
but I worked so hard on that house

                  _____

There was one future to be had by waiting it out
and another by looking elsewhere

thunder can't appease
the barometric strain of expectation
and chimes tell nothing of the future
until it is too close upon us

rumbles hunger the sky, the cloud cover,
a word I once knew to describe—

this clean break anything but "shiny"
the leg like a withered hand: "appendage"
an underground cave in an avalanche is "ingenious"
considering the dive, the inclement, the frightening paradigm

sometimes I hear a meter and what words find to put into
hardly matter
except, my god, the meaning

action, consequence, disaster

the first husbands and wives cleave closer together
and you become a symbol blinking danger
on the console: alert, alert, proximity   *fear*
one wife for another
the radar barely registers
our vow: some dim intention

LIKE WATER BUT LESS STEADY

The ferrous soil through the low-tide hemline.
Blue out further, under the sky. I would

    follow, but the world cares nothing
      for my wanting. Changes nothing.

                (Flowers open and close their faces.)

One wants to see the woman but remembers mainly the pinched-in waist,
                                             proportions.

      There and not there.   . . . ambient . . .

When removed, the body seamless, of-a-piece.
I must be still to feel her—

ooo
oo
oo

HERE HAPPY IS NO PART OF LOVE

(*birth of the second son*)

o

she is not   (in the end)   denatured   (but begins to)
like acid   body-away some under, subjacent revealed

a catalytic sizzle dissolves solvent the picture the sky with atomic bomb
cloud suddenly black, blank then

Someone shouting,
                    (a woman) she

        "go through"   "circle of fire"
"through go"   though death *go-go-go* she says *breathe*

        breathe

                        I———oh no what is that I collect, try,   I
                        lift want to set down but in parts
                        pieces no longer I *lift* want to stop
                        sit down lift I *want*   burden
                        burden burden burden   *breathe*

Organic: I cannot move.

A woman, some screaming—they say less screaming—breathe! they say—she wants to say
I am but is not hears screaming is that her? what is that *fire*? peeling away each sanity: skin,
bone like bark stripped off a slender branch inside screaming cardiac smooth muscle "you
        must breathe"

                        but who? and how to with all this screaming

it

        explodes

my body opens-in one cannot witness   is

        o

        o

At some point I started begging.

Each time in that place thinking "I must tell them" thinking "the difference between saying and thinking is they can't hear me," and would say, "I can't do this" then would sink again drowning again desperate.

Decisions were made in both places drowning and living and a woman sent out for Demerol. It was long and I went back and back and back to the place I swore I could not go. Before I knew I was there again. It came to me, became me.

And here she was fiddling and fixing the I.V. Bitter, chiding, I'd used my strength to say, "Enough!" "We hear you," they said, "we're helping." And a woman was sent for Demerol (it had been fluid). Oh I was faché and told them, told them off but the place came to me and I could say nothing.

No position, no angle, "way to manage."
Someone said, "this is the crescendo" and I thought:
fuck fuck fuck fuck, fuck-you.

then: the syringe

In snapshots—as if a disco or strobe is the syringe and I.V. suddenly tired—
snapshot: hope,   snapshot:rest   , snapshot: I . . .

                              —a muzzle descending.

                                   (not a word thought had no word snapshot: [I *will* die])

And everywhere an explosion I am inside myself which is molten clear view: there is no help shade overpass,
monumental desert.

Fear, a pure thing, is not acceptance.

    o

Behind the curtain of Demerol which made them suddenly impervious to my suffer unlike anything and made
me incoherent scream no sound to say this ocean you have poured over me is not cooling down this one bit
drowning but only some plankton morgue you thought would shut me up—

                    they said circle of fire so many times it seemed stupid I had no
choice but burn and burn and then something ungodly——what was *that*?

                                        someone said, *I see it*
                                        someone said, *crowning*

An explosion that would not move.

Circle of fire, they say.
Push, she says.

Something——the room—shifting———

". . . get the doctor."

○

[   ] is faster than I can recount what I saw was strobe again blinking series of frames in their faces and bodies a sudden new weather in the room people moving pressing a monitor to my side and a woman rushing in in street clothes everyone else in scrubs the room moving alive around me as though they have forgotten I am here dying and no one saying push it is over I think I am finally dying I . . .

     ("get Dr. Mondoni")

                                           then

"LISTEN TO ME," she says, (she looks like my midwife my husband holding my left leg just like he did for my first child and who is that stern woman purse tight across her chest like some pageant ribbon or breastplate) "you MUST push"

and I know this is not the circle of fire.
is fire. Out of, chaos.

—Perhaps a woman wrote the image of god contracting to create the world before she died as Rachel died in labor with Benjamin she named him *Ben Oni* son of my mourning a midwife herself perhaps she knew she would not breathe this fire as they tended and she screamed how Jacob had the nerve to change the name to son of my right hand—

They lower the side rail. They fumble.

And the woman: *Get Dr. Mondoni!* and someone pushes in a baby warmer I think my husband says "the head" I must push I must I hear a hot sound inside the body, a moment liquid/vapor— *Stop Screaming* someone says and I realize for the first time I am screaming—

you—   *must—*   she says

and I did did not want to die I did and feel a ripping deep turning something in what should be out this is not the circle of fire something else this is in *in* a burrowing when nothing left to burn

and the baby slides

o

o

"The truth is I did not want this baby though beautiful it almost kills me and bleeding waiting I am not safe even my bedroom ipso facto the post partum a nest like a bird with only plastic or glass slivers to build with makes one sit gingerly alive I'm not safe here there was I know technology for this for even a woman with one young child wanted more but not so soon but how can we have everything I thought it's not my place to make this absolute fuck you to whomever sperm egg zygote (God?) I can handle this but cannot, barely not, rock/rock and cover my breasts on fire with chilled cabbage leaves these monstrous bosom-rocks with carelessly cut-out holes for the huge bruise-colored nipples . . ."

is not a metaphor for, is

o

o

When they brought the baby his was my own face.

My face, survived.

Is he OK? I said a hundred times is he? where is he? why is he? yes, they said he is. He is. They just want to—
he is, they said. Beautiful, they said. Big! they said. Your husband weeping.

The face of course it is not yours, perhaps the Demerol, but that moment and even after when your husband
said what's his name? and only my own name came to mind.

Myself divided, severed,   everyone smiling.

o

5 a.m., snow, a low mustard light.

"dying is better than this" someone says in your voice no one hears

      Birthing is no— metaphor?

Lest the suckler hunger. Least.

bones under the bedclothes suffer. I every day age three and don't recall

and there is that sharp taste again like the smell of by-products, a released consequence

The smell, the mess, the literal place, on all fours like an animal—you remember nothing.
And too much.

And am I now one with other women? hardly   except perhaps my shattered
   this and this happened then   this   the is   so now you know

everything—in and out of the room see a body splayed and naked giving up—and you?

I'm sorry but there is no new place for anyone to touch me.

[NOTES AND DEDICATIONS]

My love and gratitude to Arielle Greenberg, D. A. Powell, David Trinidad and the Peer Group (John, Jeff, Patricia, and Hermine), and, of course, to Josh Goren.

"A Kind of Catastrophe" is for Josh.
"What the Living Look Like" is for Lynn Heitler.
"Endnotes for What the Living Look Like" is for my father.
"The Window Is One-Sided It Does Not Admit" is for Moses.
"Not Knowing Nijinsky or Diaghilev" is for Phyllis Rosen.
"Despite Reports, Curious George Not a Monkey, Has No Tail" is for Jeremy Mindich with thanks to Jerry Goren.
"Here Happy Is No Part of Love" is for Lynn Chapman, midwife extraordinaire.

"In Your Version of Heaven I Am Younger" refers to the crash of Swiss Air Flight 111.

The title "The Desserts Will Make You Stupid with Happiness" is borrowed from the title of a restaurant review by Hal Rubenstein in *New York Magazine.*

A trilliant is a three-sided diamond cut.

In "Here Happy Is No Part of Love" I refer to *tsimtsum,* a theory introduced by Rabbi Isaac Luria, a sixteenth-century kabbalist. *Tsimtsum,* or "the withdrawal of light," is Luria's answer to the problem of how God could have created the world when God was every-where. Luria suggests that God contracts, drawing the divine presence away from one point, thus creating a void into which the universe is manifested.

Cabbage leaves are used to ease the discomfort of postpartum engorgement. Place chilled green cabbage leaves between your breasts and bra for about twenty minutes or until leaves are wilted.

[ACKNOWLEDGMENTS]

Many thanks to the editors of the following journals in which these poems (sometimes in different versions) first appeared.

American Poetry Review: "In Your Version of Heaven I Am Younger" and "I Cannot Write Essays Will Not Be Famous"
Barrow Street: "Not Knowing Nijinsky or Diaghilev"
Can We Have Our Ball Back: "Against Disappointment"
Colorado Review: "Despite Reports, Curious George Not a Monkey, Has No Tail"
Courier: "The Twenty-Seventh Week"
Crowd: "Sonnet Non-Volta"
Diner: "The Argument Was Simple," "The Rise in the Avenue," "Viviparity," "What the Living Look Like," and "Endnotes for What the Living Look Like"
Fence: "Trying to Reassure You"
How2: "Here Happy Is No Part of Love"
Lit: "Having a Baby, Atom Bomb"
MiPoesis: "The Moon Has a Reputation for Being Fickle," "Being Marked or Obvious," and "Five Days on Fire Island or 'Marriage Opens a Panel on a Lacquered Box'"
Pleiades: A Journal of New Writing: "The Window Is One-Sided It Does Not Admit" and "What I Want You to See Is She When Not Here As in Now"
The Iowa Review: "A Kind of Catastrophe"
Salt Hill: "When I Knock on the Wall of the Next Stanza"
Washington Square: "White Wash"

"In Your Version of Heaven I Am Younger" was reprinted in *Best American Poetry 2001* (Scribner), edited by Robert Hass and David Lehman.

"Despite Reports, Curious George Not a Monkey, Has No Tail" was reprinted in *Crossroads: Journal of the Poetry Society of America*.

[ABOUT THE AUTHOR]

Rachel Zucker is a graduate of Yale and the Iowa Writers' Workshop. She is the recipient of several awards including the Center for Book Arts Award, the Barrow Street Prize, and the Strousse Award. Wesleyan published her first collection of poetry, *Eating in the Underworld,* in 2003. She lives in New York with her husband and their two sons.

For more information please visit www.rachelzucker.net